Mrs. Minister

Zenola Diggs

Mrs. Minister

Zenola Diggs

Lighthouse Press
Nashville, Tennessee 37228

Unless otherwise indicated, all Scripture quotations are taken from The Holy Bible: New International Version. Copyright 1973, 1978, 1984 by The International Bible Society. Used by permission of Zondervan Bible Publishers.

Mrs. Minister

Zenola Diggs

Mrs. Minister
ISBN 0-9703823-1-6
Copyright 2001 One Flesh Ministries, Inc.
Madison, Tennessee

Cover Design: Jennifer L. Hoffman
Printing by Omni PublisXpress
Published by
Lighthouse Press
P.O. Box 281375
Nashville, Tennessee 37228

All rights reserved. No part of this publication may be reproduced, stored in a retrieval system, or transmitted in any form or by any means-electronic, mechanical, digital, photocopy recording, or any other—except for brief quotations in printed reviews, without the prior written permission of the publisher.

Printed in the United States of America.

Acknowledgements:

I call you Jesus. My Lord and Savior. Without You, I would be NOTHING.

To my husband, my friend, my buddy, my "Mr. Minister". Min. Rodney K. Diggs. Thank you so much for being content to let me shine. You are the inspiration behind this project. You are my ministry.

To my late father, Sam Green and my sweet mother, Nancy M. Green. Daddy, I miss you. Thank you for leaving me your sense of humor and precious memories. Mama, I thought I'd never say this, but thanks for not sparing the rod, for running the boys off and for pushing me to do all of the things that would make you proud. I love you!

To my siblings, Mr. & Mrs. Samuel L. (Wanda) Green and Onrea Green. I love ya!

To my extended family, the Green and Davis descendants of Jonesville, Louisiana. I love y'all. Not to forget, the Diggs family as well.

To my awesomely anointed Pastor and his most gracious wife, Bishop Joseph W. and Dr. Diane (Greer) Walker, III. Wow! What examples of true ministry and support you have been for me, personally. How can I say, "I love you!" any better than, "I love you!" I love you too, Mt. Zion Baptist Church-Nashville!

To Bishop Odis A. Floyd, Rev. Russell McReynolds and Rev. Alonzo E. Vincent. Thank you for your pastoral guidance and friendship during the most important years of my life.

To the rest of my dear friends, thank you for being genuine.

Table of Contents

Introduction

What Has God Told You To Do? 1

Honoring The Covenant 8

The Virtuous Married Woman 12

Tools for Building A Strong Marriage 21

Praying Power 30
(A Husband's Prayer)

Do You Like What You See? 34

Murder, Adultery, Divorce 39

"Dear Abby" 47

A Humble Wife's Prayer 55

Find The Meaning In Ministering To Your Spouse 57

Another Tenth Commandment 63

Appendix 66
(Helps & Referral Agencies)

Notes 70

About The Author 71

Introduction

There are so many reasons why I have decided to write this book, Mrs. Minister. However, the one most important reason that comes to mind is because I want any person who reads this book to be blessed and their marriage enriched as God has purposed it to happen.

To read Mrs. Minister is to read a book about the spiritual knowledge I have gained from my own personal devotional time, biblical research and life experiences. My inspiration has come from numerous conversations and counseling sessions I have had with many women (and men) just like you and even some of you perhaps. Most of all, I am constantly provoked and mainly inspired by the relationship I have with my husband, Minister Rodney K. Diggs of nine years.

Six years ago, my husband and I moved to Nashville, Tennessee from Michigan seeking a change in careers. I have never lived more than forty-five miles away from home before in my life! God was definitely doing a new thing in my life, especially in my marriage. What an adjustment I was going to have to make! A new state, few if any friends and very little family for miles around. My husband Rodney had always been quite an adventurer and socialite; therefore, he was in Heaven while I wallowed in my own personal Hell. What's more, I left the church experience I had grown to know and love back home. My husband and I had found and joined a church, but I found myself still lost and hungry for God's word and guidance. It wasn't home. I wasn't being spiritually fed. Needless to say, this took a huge toll on our marriage.

In 1997 the Lord gave my husband and me a ministry as lay-members at our new church home, the Mt. Zion Baptist Church-Nashville. We began our service to the church as lay members, teaching a weekly Marriage Enrichment Sunday School class, later to receive God's call to the joint ministry of Marriage Enrichment.

Four years later we are still teaching Marriage Enrichment classes and conducting pre and post marital counseling, seminars and conferences at one of the largest and fastest growing churches in the state of Tennessee as well as through One Flesh Ministries, Inc. Our personal ministry allows us to further expand the ministry of Marriage Enrichment wherever the Holy Spirit leads us. What an awesome God we serve! Not only is God healing our marriage daily, he has put us in divine position to help other marriages heal globally.

I quickly learned though I have a joint ministry with my husband, there are some very specific things that God requires of me; 1) maintain integrity, 2) follow my husband as long as he follows Christ and 3) not to be ashamed of the Gospel. Following these three basic principles has allowed me to effectively minister to my own marriage and maintain my peace of mind.

If you are a Mrs., then you are definitely in position to Minister. A clergical collar or the validation of mortal man does not define your God-given appointment. Christian, covenant marriage is a divine calling. You are simply called to serve-to minister to your marriage and to your spouse. "Wives submit yourselves unto your own husbands, as unto the Lord" (Ephesians 5:22, KJV).

Learn to do what God has asked, Mrs. Minister and may your marriage be blessed!

What Has God Told You To Do?

"Leave her alone," said Jesus..."She has done a beautiful thing to me." Mark 14:6-9 (KJV)

It really doesn't matter how many books a person may read about marriage and relationships, whether the book is written from a Christian or secular perspective. It doesn't matter one bit how many times you declare you are a loosed woman or an empowered man as the result of attending a sensational conference or soul stirring convention. If you have not made up in your mind that you will be the woman or man God has need of, any effort you make now or from now on will be fruitless. If you have not made up in your mind to surrender to the Holy Spirit that dwells within your innermost being, then the price you paid for hotel accommodations, the gas you burned to get to the super- dome complex, the T-shirt you bought and the book you had personally signed by the author are all for naught. People who find themselves hurting, confused and frustrated at one time or another are in need of an anointed word from God. We want the truth because it is the truth that makes us free. Notice I said "we" and "us". This minister is not exempt.

It has become evident that so many couples who find themselves struggling minute by minute, hour by hour, day by day, year after year (you get the picture?) is because they have failed to surrender themselves totally and unselfishly to God. There has to be an absolute surrender to God's will and a conscientious effort to yield to a mind transformation (Romans 12:2). Without this kind of surrender, it will be virtually impossible for the Holy Spirit to bring forth an about face to your situation.

A few years ago, I was sharing with a dear friend and confidant my frustrations with my stepson and his new wife who had come to live with my husband and me. The plan was that they were only going to stay long enough "to get themselves straight." Well, needless to say, days turned into weeks, weeks turned into months. My patience was beyond worn thin with everyone at our address. I even discovered that it is quite possible to even get on your own nerves. I know I certainly was getting on mine. My young daughter-in-law and I just couldn't seem to see eye to eye when it came down to facing the facts of how to be a virtuous woman, if you will. I had come from a tough-love, yet spoiled-Yes, I'm admitting it, upbringing where a young lady was taught to be a lady at all times. How clean you kept house, yourself and how well you managed your household clearly defined womanhood in my mama's household. And by all means, kept your hair done, nails (fingers and toes) polished and clothes ironed!

Do you think my daughter-in-law was about to invest in my self-indulgent course in *Domestics 101?* Honey, NO! I just knew in my mind that she was rebelling just to be rebellious. I even tried winning her husband over to my points of view -thinking all the while he would become a positive and much expected influence in her life. This was a big no-no for real. Though my husband and I had taught a series of marriage enrichment courses for about a year at the time, I hadn't fully grasped hold of the Genesis 2:24 concept, *"For this reason a man will leave his father and mother and be united to his wife, and they will become one flesh."* After all, these folks were in my house! Don't get me wrong, please, I loved them; I just didn't have the tolerance for them. Allow me to be honest.

While I was "working" on my daughter-in-law, my husband was "working" on his son. You see, this was *his* son, *his* flesh and blood and he wasn't going to stand by and passively watch his son hit what he perceived as rock bottom. Primarily because of the marital blunder his son seemed to have so obviously made. Needless to say, since we were operating on the "one flesh" principle, we were going to stick together on this one. What we hadn't realized was even though my son and daughter-in-law were under our roof whether we liked it, despised it, rebuked it or whatever, they too were one flesh.

My girlfriend Lisa came over to our home to visit one evening, and of course, I just had to vent. Lisa turned to me after letting me purge myself for about an hour and deliberately as she knew how, spoke these words to me, "If you and your husband will just allow him to become the man he needs to be, his wife will become the woman she needs to be" and vise-versa. It was after that moment, I realized how foolishly we were behaving. God then spoke to me and said, "You just do what you are supposed to do!" Ignorantly, I tried to convince God that I was not the one with the problem. It was all of them and none of me. The Lord, God spoke it again. This time louder, clearer, like a mother giving that final warning to come into the house before the street lights came on. "You just do what you are supposed to do!" Quickly, I began to make a mind transformation. All right then God! Ouch! I hear you! I hear you!

How many times have you missed an opportunity to work on you because you were too engrossed in searching out and exposing the imperfections in someone else's life, namely your spouse's? I tell couples all of the time, women in particular, since these tendencies are more apparent among our gender, no matter what your spouse does, God has given you specific instructions that he expects you to follow. First, as a woman of God, and secondly as a wife (1Peter, 3:1-6). Imagine standing before the pearly gates on judgment day. Your husband, your children, your closest friend, not even your Pastor will be able to stand with you or speak on your behalf. God will hold you accountable for the work he has entrusted to you and you alone.

The God we serve is not a God of suggestions; He is a God of direct commands and clear expectations. God does not suggest His will be done, He commands His will be done with deliberate consequences if we choose to do the contrary. When you have decided to go against your own opposition and yield to the voice of God, He will release you from the things that are causing you strife. Your efforts will begin to bear good fruit and will be made evident by the lives you touch. Walk according to God's will and He will say to your stumbling blocks, "Leave her alone...she has done a beautiful thing unto to me."

Reflections:

- *Are there any specific attitudes that need to be adjusted in your life?*

- *How would you and your relationship with your spouse, children and extended family change if you would absolutely surrender to God's will?*

- *What are you willing to do to bring about positive change to your situation?*

Motivational Scriptures:

Search me, O God, and know my heart; test me and know my anxious thoughts. See if there is any offensive way in me, and lead me in the way everlasting. (Psalm 139:23-24)

Trust in the Lord with all your heart and lean not on your own understanding; in all your ways acknowledge him, and he will make your paths straight. (Proverbs 3:5-6)

Therefore, I urge you, brothers, in view of God's mercy, to offer your bodies as living sacrifices, holy and pleasing to God-this is your spiritual act of worship. Do not conform any longer to the pattern of this world, but be transformed by the renewing of your mind. Then you will be able to test and approve what God's will is-his good, pleasing and perfect will. (Romans 12:1-2)

Honoring the Covenant

In order to have a Covenant Marriage, it is important for Christian couples to fully understand the meaning of Covenant as it pertains to marriage. Most of us know and understand Covenant to mean a pact or promise made between two or more parties. More specifically, an expression of commitment and care for each other that mirrors God's love and care for us. Have you ever truly paid attention to the promises of God as they are presented in the Bible? If so, you will notice that before God made a promise of any kind, He always made reference to the Covenant, and He still does. Remembering the marriage covenant is important. Why? Because the world would have you believe that two people, living harmoniously together until death do them part is a mere fantasy. Get out of here! Who does that? Look at the grocery checkout line tabloids, television and other media images of what appears to be great relationships gone sour. Well, if the rich and famous can't buy a lasting relationship, then what is the destiny of the not so famous and so-called nameless?

Just take a look around your neighborhood, and yes, even the faith community. There the enemy is again; trying to convince us that what God has joined together can be put asunder. In a great number of these instances, you will find people who have failed to honor the Marriage Covenant.

So, what does honoring the Covenant in general terms mean? Honoring the Marriage Covenant means to offer each other steadfast loyalty, forgiveness, empathy, and commitment to resolving conflict effectually in order to motivate one another to grow spiritually. However, where there is no commitment, there is no growth. Entering into a marriage covenant means that a husband and wife will toil to love one another without demands and stipulations that never ceases (Lamentations 3:22).

Covenant does not mean that I will give love and receive love as long as I meet the expectations of my spouse. Covenant means I will give love and receive love from my spouse whether either of us deserves it or not. After all, isn't that the same kind of unconditional, unreserved, consummate love God has for each one of us? (Romans 8:38-39). "It's perplexing", you say? "You don't know the man or woman I have to live with day in and day out", you say? Know this- God's grace is sufficient to overcome any struggles we may endure. Covenant marriage is not possible without God. "And by this all men will know that you are my disciples, if you love one another" (John 13:35).

The Bible records seven types of covenants made by God. A promise and a specific sign characterizes each covenant made between God and man. We should think of the Marriage Covenant in these terms. God's promise is, "…Therefore what God has joined together, let man not separate." (Matt. 19:6). The sign of this covenant is a marriage that lasts a lifetime.

A covenant is an unconditional promise. Throughout history God has made covenants with his people- He keeps his end of the bargain, even when we fail to keep ours. However, when we fail to live up to our end, just like in marriage, there are consequences we must face. Here are several covenants found in the Bible:

Name and Reference	God's Promise	Sign
In Eden **Genesis 3:15**	Satan and mankind will be enemies	Pain of childbirth
Noah **Genesis 9:8-17**	God would never again destroy the earth with a flood	Rainbow
Abraham **Genesis 15:12-21; 17:1-14**	Abraham's descendants would become a great nation if they obeyed God. God would be their God forever.	Smoking firepot and blazing torch
At Mount Sinai **Exodus 19:5,6**	Israel would be God's special people, a holy nation. But they would have to keep their part of the covenant-obedience	The exodus
The Priesthood **Numbers 25:10-13**	Aaron's descendants would be priests forever	The Aaronic priesthood
David **2 Samuel 7:13; 25:5**	Salvation would come through David's line through the birth of the Messiah	David's line continued and the Messiah was born a descendant of David
New Covenant **Romans 10:9-10**	Forgiveness and salvation are available through faith in Christ.	Christ's resurrection

Source: Life Application Bible (NIV)

The Virtuous Married Woman

I Peter 3:1-6 (Narrated Bible); "Wives, in the same way be submissive to your husbands so that, if any of them do not believe the word, they may be won over without words by the behavior of their wives, when they see the purity and reverence of your lives. Your beauty should not come from outward adornment, such as braided hair and the wearing of gold jewelry and fine clothes. Instead, it should be that of your inner self, the unfading beauty of a gently and quiet spirit, which is of great worth in God's sight. For this is the way the holy women of the past who put their hope in God used to make themselves beautiful." They were submissive *(honored his obligation as head of the household)* to their own husbands, like Sarah, who obeyed Abraham and called him her master *(lord in lower case means she reverenced him)*.

We are Sarah's daughters if we do what is right and do not give way to fear.

A VIRTUOUS WIFE KNOWS HOW TO WIN HER HUSBAND OVER WITH SUBMISSION

When a man feels genuinely respected by his wife, he is won over to honor God and His word. This is the basis for mutual submission. When you and your husband are in submission to God, submitting to one another becomes effortless. What is submission? Submission means to line up according to rank or to be under authority. A common misapprehension that most women (and men) have about submission is a wife who submits to her husband becomes inferior, passive and powerless. Nothing can be farther from the truth. Scripture teaches us in Ephesians 5:24: "Now as the church submits to Christ, so also wives should submit to their husbands in everything." Therefore, as the church relates to Christ in submission, the wife is to relate to her husband in the same manner. Let's not overlook the preceding scripture, Ephesians 5:21: "Submit to one another out of reverence for Christ." Allow one another to function in the "rank" God has placed you in. The leadership of the household falls on the shoulders of the husband. I know you may be thinking to yourself this is all well and good if your husband is able to make sound decisions, is not weak, and has leadership qualities. Yes, I know that there are some men who seem to be clueless in these areas, perhaps even worse. There are some wives who are forced to make independent decisions about virtually everything in the home and pertaining to the family in general. However, as soon as your husband shows one ounce of God-fearing initiative, submit to his leadership. Trust me, he will appreciate your new outlook on life. Before you know it, you will find yourself noticing what your husband does right more often than what he's doing wrong. When you do, tell him. Follow your husband as he follows Christ. Mutual submission can and will result. Most importantly, remember what God has asked you to do.

Once you have the submission principle down, you will be well on your way to winning him over. Joshua said, "As for me and my house, we will serve the Lord." How are you representing your household in the eyes of the Lord? If your husband provides for the house, is it too much to ask, virtuous woman, that you make it a home?

A VIRTUOUS WIFE KNOWS AND UNDERSTANDS HER REAL BEAUTY COMES FROM WITHIN

How many of you women out there know that your greatest strength is not in what you drape on your body? Of course, the hair more or less is nice, the outfit worn decently and in order is wonderful, and you've got more karats than Bugs Bunny, that's wonderful, BUT WHAT DOES YOUR ATTITUDE LOOK LIKE? IS YOUR PERSONALITY BEAUTIFUL AND SOMETHING MARVELOUS TO BEHOLD? Learn to honor your uniqueness. Do not wait for a man to make you feel complete or to give you instructions on how to be a lady. If your man has to spend time teaching you things about womanhood, you may soon weary him and he will feel he has no use for you. Pretty much the same way you feel when you have to educate him in the areas of masculinity. If you truly are unsure and have not fully matured in this area, try seeking the counsel and input of positive, God-fearing, female mentors who possess the wifely and biblically based qualities you aspire to obtain. Strive to obtain beauty internally as well as externally.

Years ago there weren't any "Woman Thou Art Loosed" conferences, or books that addressed female empowerment such as *The Lady, Her Lover, Her Lord* by Bishop T.D. Jakes or *The Power of a Praying Wife,* by Stormie Omartian. However, it seemed our mothers, grandmothers and women who took a part in rearing us in whatever capacity had something greater. It was called "Mother's Wit" and a Bible. Allow me to make this statement clearer to you, COMMON SENSE AND THE WORD OF GOD.

Of course, times have changed tremendously from generation to generation, and I do not mean to imply that everything Ma'dear practiced in the house with Papa would work today. No, there's nothing wrong at all with resources and present day inspiration to aid us in reaching our ultimate spiritual level. However, it is just as important to remember the something that we have within us, something in our ancestral blood-lines that should spark the flame of common sense. If nothing else, there is something in the blood of Jesus Christ our Lord and Savior that runs in our veins. It is the Holy Spirit that leads and guides us daily.

Take time to yield to God's presence if you feel God is not near to you in the midst of your circumstances. Stop where you are right now and invite His awesome spirit into your life. He's just a prayer away.

A VIRTUOUS WIFE IS MINDFUL OF WHAT TO SAY AND DO

A woman that knows the appropriate things to say and do at the appropriate time can always get her man's attention. Delilah was able to seduce Samson because she filled his voids. When Mrs. Samson was not meeting Samson's expectations, Delilah made her move, saying all of the right things and stroking Samson's ego.

A Christian woman should always remember that God created man in His image. That includes His mental psyche as well. God created man for several reasons and divine appointments, but most importantly he created man to praise Him. Then God realized no one was present to praise man. God gave Adam a job and means to provide, and then he created Eve for Adam. Woman for Man.

Virtuous women of God, we must come to realize that the power of life and death are in our tongues (Prov. 18:21). Watch the things you say. You just may speak those negative murmurings into existence. If you tell God He's your doctor, then your body will be healed. If you tell Him He is your comforter, He'll be there when your days and nights are lonely. If you tell Him He is your provider, he will be your Jehovah Jireh. He will always be more than enough!

Now, on the other hand, if you tell your husband he is lazy, he'll be reluctant to demonstrate initiative. If you tell him he is so stupid and silly, he will continue to behave like a clown. If you tell him all the things your mama and your sister- girls said you don't have to put up with, then you won't learn to be patient enough to wait for divine change. What's more, you may find yourself spending more time with your mama and sister-girls than God and your husband will be able to stand. If you continue to tell your sons they'll never amount to anything-they are the spitting image of the men you despise, then who will they model themselves after -the feminine side of you? God forbid! Bear in mind, our young men have the potential to become future husbands and fathers. If you continue this nonsense, then you've opened up an entirely different can of worms that must be dealt with later in life. Perhaps sooner than later.

Be cautious of what you say and do! In the same way God loves to be praised, worshipped, adored, magnified, exalted and welcomed into our secret and most intimate places, so does your husband- expected and unexpected. Let him in. He will prove to be a blessing to you!

Men react to praise as well as to the negativity that comes out of our mouths. We have the ability to speak life and death into their lives until he becomes what we say!

<u>Key Points to Remember</u>

1. A Virtuous Wife Knows How To Win Her Husband Over With Submission
2. A Virtuous Wife Understands Real Beauty Comes From Within
3. A Virtuous Wife Is Mindful of What To Say and Do

God Bless You Virtuous Wives of God and Man!!

"Tools for Building a Strong Marriage"

When faced with the question, "What does it take to have a happy marriage?" We know from experience, a happy marriage just doesn't happen, it takes plenty of work. We have found this to be especially true now that my husband Rodney and I have answered the call to teach and counsel numerous couples with very diverse backgrounds. With these cultural, ethnically and geographically identified sociological traits come a plethora of cultural, geographical and spiritual issues. If we as Christian couples are not careful, these kinds of traits can be more of a detriment than a blessing for a relationship meant to last from this day forward. "A pure walk before the Lord does not allow for the darkness of anger and resentment" (I John 2:9-11).

Wives Know Your Husbands

Who can love and support a husband who is more like a stranger than a mate to us? Wives you need to know what turns your husband off as well as what turns him on. If he won't verbally communicate with you, pay attention to his actions. They will speak much louder than words. Your husband is made in the image of God, therefore his God-man needs to be praised and adored just like your heavenly father longs for praise and adoration.

Learn to bless instead of curse your husband's actions and deeds whether they are intentional or otherwise. After all, when we curse our mates, we curse God. Motivate your husband to be a blessing in your life if that is really what you desire.

Your husband needs to know that he is a priority in your life. I hear a devoted mother saying, "But what about the children?" "They need me more than he does right now." "He's a grown man and can do things for himself. The kids can't." Oh, I hear this so often! Normally, I do not minister in areas where I have little or no experience, simply because that's a dangerous place. I do not have biological children who live with me, so let me tell you something I heard from a very wise woman. Be careful of putting your children's needs before your husband's needs too often. Children are stronger and more adaptable than we think. A woman does well when she is in tune with that little boy inside her husband, longing to be nurtured. There's also a child in him that needs your attention.

Your children will not perish if you teach them delayed gratification. Child abuse kills children. Teaching them to wait does not. If you are a mother who jumps at every whimper, every adolescent demand, every cry for attention, your children will soon learn to manipulate you. No, I am not advocating child negligence by any means. Let's be clear on that. The point I am making is simply do not influence your husband and children to compete for your affection. Make no room for resentment. Learn to balance your time between your husband and your kids. No, it's not easy, but think about it for just a second. If you attend to your husband the way God intends, he will eventually gain motivation and strength. Attend to your husband. He may just willfully begin to assist you with the children in their times of need. If you find yourself needing additional help in this area, seek resources that will assist you with time management skills and how to balance your home, family and career. Most importantly pray without ceasing.

With God's help, the children will learn to honor your relationship as husband and wife. They will come to realize that Daddy needs a little time with Mommy in order to maintain peace in our home and for our family to be happy. What's more, the children will see that Mommy is sticking to her guns and I'm not getting my way until she decides I will. Your husband will be motivated to be more supportive and take advantage of more quality time with you.   Men also need other strong Christian men to spiritually challenge their Christian mentality and accountability to his wife and family. You will do well to encourage your husband to seek other strong Christian men to fellowship with. Give him some breathing room every once in a while. He will return to you and the family refreshed and less stressed.

It is a blessing that so many churches are now incorporating strong, male ministries and Christian men fellowship groups locally and throughout the nation. Thank God for Bishop T.D. Jake's Manpower Conferences, Promise Keepers and the New Mentality Men's Ministry at my home church and others like these. I think it would be safe to say that a common misconception is that most men, especially in the African-American community for some reason or another have become increasingly apathetic as it pertains to being responsible husbands and fathers. Thank God, the truth of the matter is at least, Christian men are becoming more animate about diligently seeking God for direction. As a result, these men are becoming spiritual role models for those who have not caught on just yet.

A wife can be many things to her husband, but let the truth be told; she cannot provide the masculine support a man of God needs. Remember the story of David and Bathsheba? David's relationships with Bathsheba would never have gotten off the ground if David had pre-established an accountable relationship with Jonathan. As wives, it would be wise to embrace such friendships rather than resent the time our husbands spend with other men of God. Of course if your husband has negative influences in his life, it is up to the wife to caringly speak up about his choice of friends and the way he spends his time. Be mindful to pave the way for conversations with prayer. A 1Peter 3:4 woman wins her husband over with a quiet and gentle spirit. Your husband should be happy to come home to you and his family, not regretting the very moment he turns the key.

Husbands Know Your Wives

Do your best to understand her language, her habits and her moods. What a challenge! With God's help it can be done. Are you a teacher, a fixer, or a sounding board? When is it appropriate to be all or none of the above? God's design for man is to be a helper and Godly influence, but never a know it all. Always an initiator, but never an oppressor. Always a provider and protector, but never one who stifles. Always a friend and lover, but never a jail warden.

I am reminded of an article I read some time ago that made reference to certain breakdowns that occur in our marriages. The breakdowns in general were referred to as *"missed cues"*. The writer reflected that "missed cues" occur when we find ourselves blaming and making excuses for not being in the right place at the right time to tackle those things that challenge our relationships. The core of the problem can be interpreted into a simple feeling of having your dance partner continue to miss his cue once the music is played. Tragically, the core issues are kept silent among partners. Perhaps because they are not quite understood and even more difficult to effectively discuss. You've heard the saying; "It takes two to tango" I'm sure. So what happens when we fail to get our dance steps in sync? What happens when you find yourself spun around on the dance floor only to return to your starting position and find your partner has disappeared? You will look ridiculous dancing alone. Seek to walk in agreement with your spouse. "Can two walk together, except they be agreed?" (Amos 3:3). God posed this question to a rebellious Israel whom he loved. Are you rebelling against walking in agreement with the one you love? Are you rebelling against your marriage-the very institution that God has ordained?

An important lesson my husband Rodney and I try to instill within the Christian couples we come in contact with is this; *If you are the man or woman GOD has intended you to be, your mate will be the man or woman you expect him or her to be.* No one knows how to instinctively have a strong marriage. This is something that has to be learned.

As Christian couples, it is always wise to know God's plan as you pray and seek counsel. Proverbs 11:14 says, "For lack of guidance a nation falls, but many advisers make victory sure." Stay open to wise counsel and pray for wisdom to know the difference. May God continue to bless your marriage as you continue to build upon a strong foundation.

Reflections:

    Virtually every morning before my husband and I rush out of the door and off to work or begin to attend to our weekend commitments, we make it our spiritual business to pray and have devotional time with one another. Whether it is a passage of scripture or excerpt from an inspirational book we have chosen from our personal library, we have found by doing this, our marriage has been tremendously strengthened. Take time to pray and enter into God's presence, together.

Most couples are not comfortable praying together. One partner may be fine with praying aloud and the other isn't. If either of these scenarios or others similar to ones presented apply to your marriage, pray that God will teach you how to mutually touch and agree. Start off with copying and posting your favorite scriptures in areas of your home (the bathroom mirror, refrigerator, near entry ways, etc.) as a constant reminder of God's word. Perhaps pre-written prayers like the ones shared in this book or ones you and your husband have personally written for your marriage can become spiritual anthems for your household. Gently encourage your husband to pray for you and your children (if you have them) as the spiritual leader of the family. Whatever the manner in which you choose to do it, make a conscientious effort to pray as a couple. Sure, this may take a little time, but won't it be worth the wait?

In this modern age of technology, if you miss morning prayer at home, send a "knee-mail" (a term used for an emailed prayer message) to your spouse if you can. Before you know it, the both of you will begin to look forward to prayer and devotion as a means of spending quality time together.

Praying Power
(From *The Power of a Praying Husband*)

Lord, I pray that You would establish in me and **(wife's name**) bonds of love that cannot be broken.

Show me how to love my wife in an ever-deepening way that she can clearly perceive. May we have mutual respect and admiration for each other so that we can become and remain one another's greatest friend, champion, and unwavering support. Where love has been diminished, lost, destroyed, or buried under hurt and disappointment, put it back in our hearts. Give us strength to hold on to the good in our marriage, even in those times when one of us doesn't feel love.

Enable my wife and me to forgive each other quickly and completely. Specifically I lift up to You

(name any area where forgiveness is needed). Help us to "be kind to one another, tenderhearted, forgiving," the way You are for us (Ephesians 4:32). Teach us to overlook the faults and weaknesses of the other. Give us a sense of humor, especially as we deal with hard issues of life.

Unite us in faith, beliefs, standards and morality, and mutual trust. Help us to be of the same mind, to move together in harmony, and quickly come to mutual agreements about our finances, our children, how we spend our time, and any other decisions that need to be made. Where we are in disagreement and this has caused strife, I pray You would draw us together on the issues. Adjust our perspectives to align with yours. Make our communication open and honest so that we avoid misunderstandings.

May we have the grace to be tolerant of each other's faults and, at the same time, have the willingness to change. I pray that we will not live two separate lives, but instead walk together as a team. Remind us to take time for one another so that our marriage will be a source of happiness, peace, and joy for us both.

Lord, I pray that You would protect our marriage from anything that would destroy it. Take out of our lives anyone who would come between us or tempt us. Help us to immediately recognize and resist temptation when it presents itself. I pray that no other relationship either of us have had in the past, will rob us of anything in our relationship now. Sever all unholy ties in both of our lives. May there never any adultery or divorce in our future to destroy what You, Lord, have put together. Help us to never cast aside the whole relationship just because it has developed a nonworking part. I pray that we will turn to You-the Designer-to fix it and get it operating the way it was intended.

Teach us to seek each other's well being first, as You have commanded in Your Word (I Corinthians 10:24). We want to keep You at the center of our marriage and not expect from each other what only You can give. Where either of us have unrealistic expectations of the other, open our eyes to see it. May we never waver in our commitment and devotion to You and to one another, so that this marriage will become all You designed it to be.[1]

In Jesus' Name, Amen.

Do You Like What You See?

Many of us at one time or another have been faced with the poignant and somewhat bold question, "Do You Like What You See?" We have been approached with this question in one form or another whether we were dating, contemplating an engagement, newly married or have been married for some time. Perhaps it was when you were about to go on a night out on the town, and you put on your best outfit. You wanted to make sure that your date was impressed. Perhaps you caught him or her staring with hope in their eyes from across a crowded room. We spend time with one another and in spending that intimate time, we begin to learn more about our mates as the days progress. What's more, we begin to take a closer, more critical look.

The things that used to amuse us now seem to somehow

and inevitably make us frown in discontent. The jokes that used to tickle our funny bones now irritate us as if we just hit that same funny bone on some sharp, protruding object. The little things about him or her that used to appear so very endearing, have now become distorted beyond recognition and just downright ugly.

Why has all of the sudden, your mate, your precious gift from God, has now become a booby prize of sorts in your eyes? Perhaps it is because somewhere along the line of honor and cherish you've become disconnected, dissatisfied, distanced and distracted and your mate has become just plain "Dissed" (**Dis**-respected, **Dis**-missed, **Dis**-qualified and **Dis**-honored) by you. So if this is supposed to be an *"one-flesh"* relationship, someone please tell me how I ended up with this so-called flop of a person? The answer is simple; God simply puts challenges in our lives to teach us how to love with *His* kind of love. A God kind of love. Nothing wavering.

Let's put all of this into perspective. Remember when you first became a Christian? I mean a fully dedicated, committed, sold out for Christ kind of saint? No one could turn you around. No one could tell you God was not good. No one could keep you from Bible study, Sunday school, morning, afternoon and Sunday night church services. All in the same 24 hours! Then suddenly, something happened. Without warning, those things that used to influence you have started to creep up again; you began questioning God when the things you've been asking for didn't seem to materialize soon enough. Now you no longer have a hunger for Bible study every week. Sunday school is for kids and who needs an all day church service? You are content with "Bedside Baptist" with "Reverend Pillow" and First Lady "Sister Sheets" officiating. What used to be so engaging about the Lord has now become passé, but you expect your mate, the person who has been presented to you in God's image to meet all of your frivolous criteria.

Conceivably, this may be an exaggerated point, however, the one million dollar question begs to be answered, "Are you meeting all of God's criteria?" Is God pleased when he looks at you? Do you really deserve more than what you are receiving from your relationship when you are not willing to give God what He requires of you? You do know that God holds us to a higher standard, do you not? (Luke 12:48). What's your final answer? In your time of study and meditation, read Ephesians 5:21-32. Actually, this is a more advised lesson for the Christ-centered husband. God is instructing man on how to treat their wives with the same adoration as God does the church. Yet, both parties have their fair share of responsibility within the marriage.

The Apostle Paul teaches us that regardless if your mate is doing what you perceive to be his or her part in the relationship; there are still some things that God has deposited in you and you alone. " I wish that all men were as I am. But each man has his own gift from God; one has this gift, another has that." (I Corin. 7:7, NIV)   Unleash your gifts in order that they may be a positive and healing influence in your marriage. Before long, you will see those little intolerances that had you bound in your relationship healed, delivered and set free. Now when you are faced with the question, "Do you like what you see?" The answer will be a resounding Yes! Because now you're looking at your mate through God's eyes, not your own. Consequently, God will be pleased as he looks at you and so will your mate.

Reflections:

- *Of all the things your mate does, what is the one thing that you are not willing to tolerate another day?*

- *Recall the ways in which God has extended mercy and grace unto you.*

- *Why do we expect so much more grace for ourselves than we are willing to extend to others?*

- *Do you spend more time concentrating on what's wrong with your mate than what's right?*

Murder, Adultery, Divorce

Recently, as I was preparing to teach a Vacation Bible School lesson to the adults at my church, God revealed something to me about the subject Murder, Adultery and Divorce. The lesson I was teaching on this particular evening dealt specifically with the sanctity of human life and marriage. The lesson plan explained how we show respect for life by demonstrating that we recognize the sanctity of human life and of marriage by doing nothing to violate that sanctity. (Ex. 20:13-14). The Hebrew verb for kill found in Exodus 20:13 means to murder. Simple enough, I thought, but as I began to dig deeper into the VBS leader's guide, there were several other scripture references that went along with the lesson. The sub-topic that followed the initial topic was *Attitudes That Affect* (the sanctity of human life and marriage). The scripture references were Matthew 5:27-28.

We will examine these scriptures more closely in a moment.

While I studied, I began to notice the subheadings in the Bible that preceded each passage of scripture as found in the NIV Study Bible. The subheading that precedes verses 21 through 26 in the fifth chapter of Matthew is Murder. The subheading that precedes verses 27 through 30 of the same chapter of Matthew is *Adultery*. Finally, the subheading that precedes verses 31 through 32 is Divorce.

Hmmm, I thought to myself, this is interesting. Why did Matthew divide the text in this way? Why are the subheadings found in this order? At that moment, God revealed to me that this is the succession of how events occur in our relationships. Specifically, in our marriages if we allow Satan to have control. Take a closer look and perhaps you will agree. Whenever you have a relationship that takes a turn for the worst, usually the first thing that happens is a "dying off" affect. Things such as emotions, intimacy, communication and love for one another in general begins to diminish because something has died somewhere in the relationship. How did it die? It was *murdered*. Who murdered it? Maybe it was you. Maybe it was your spouse. Maybe you both had your hands on the trigger and fired together. Whatever the case may be, that thing or things that used to keep your relationship alive and fruitful have died off.

When things begin to die off, our natural tendency is to seek life in alternate places. When we place this reasoning in perspective with the marital relationship, the results bend towards *Adultery*. Mind you, we haven't buried what is dead; we have just allowed it to lie around and fester while we search to find life in something (or someone) else. My God, what a revelation! Remember Matthew 5:27-28? Jesus tells us through the scriptures these are the attitudes and thought processes that affect the sanctity of human life and marriage. The mind of an adulterer. One who ventures outside of the covenant.

According to Jesus, verse 28 says he who looks at a woman (or man) lustfully, not a passing glance, but with willful desire, a stare that is calculated that stirs up sinful sexual desire is a form of adultery even if it is only "in his heart." In the context of this passage of scripture, Jesus tells the disciples that anyone who divorces his wife, except for marital unfaithfulness, causes her to become an adulteress, and anyone who marries the divorced woman commits adultery (Matt. 5:32). This is the lesson taught by Jesus to those who thought it acceptable to put his wife away (divorce her) for ludicrous reasons and those who sought to entrap Him with foolish questions.

In his book, *Loving Your Marriage Enough to Protect It*, author Jerry B. Jenkins explains the issue of adultery better than any author's work I have ever read. Jenkins shares the theory, "If the Bible deals with this modern day issue, it had better do it in a sophisticated, up-to-date way or no one will pay attention."[2]

Reference is made to Leviticus 20:10. Adulterers are put to death. Remember Matthew 5:27-28? Lust is adultery. Who is guilty among us? The stories found in John 8:3-11 lets us know that there is such a thing as forgiveness and we can start over.

> *The teachers of the law and the Pharisees brought in a woman caught in adultery. They made her stand before the group and said to Jesus, "Teacher, this woman was caught in the act of adultery. In the Law Moses commanded us to stone such women. Now what do you say?" They were using this question as a trap, in order to have a basis for accusing him.*

But Jesus bent down and started to write on the ground with his finger. When they kept on questioning him, he straightened up and said to them, "If any one of you is without sin, let him be the first to throw a stone at her. Again he stooped down and wrote on the ground.

At this, those who heard began to go away one at a time, the older ones first, until only Jesus was left, with the woman and still standing there. Jesus straightened up and asked her, "Woman, where are they? Has no one condemned you?"
"No one, sir," she said. "Then neither do I condemn you, Jesus declared. "Go now and leave your life of sin."

Jenkins counsels his audience not to make the same mistake of assuming that Jesus was condoning adultery. Jesus called her adultery sin and told her to leave her life of sin. The irony Jenkins so eloquently illustrates in this eighth chapter of John is that Jesus says the one "among you" without sin should cast the first stone. We are challenged to recognize that there was one among them who was without sin. It was Jesus himself and he chose not to cast a stone. Thank God for grace and mercy!

So now what happens when the stench of this dead relationship becomes more than we can bear? Someone finally decides to take time to bury it. A deep hole is dug; the dirt is thrown back over it, a few words are said, if any, and it's left to be virtually remembered no more. The couple is *Divorced*, physically and emotionally. So often, couples or individuals who are contemplating the act of divorcing their spouse will share with my husband and me how they are struggling with this issue. The first thing that naturally comes to mind to a Christian at any level of maturity of his or her Christian walk is God hates divorce. That is absolutely correct. What we do have to understand is that God's insistence that couples stay together once they are married does not imply that people stay in cancerous marriages with no recourse but to stick it out.

By all means, if you are in an abusive relationship, get out now! Love has nothing to do with that. Yes, God hates divorce (Mal. 2:13-16), but it is also quite clear that the Lord God loves each and every one of his children, even those who are going through marital difficulties. It is not the divorce per se that God hates, it is the hurt, alienation and disruption it causes His children.

It would not be fair to say that those persons who have gone through with divorces have failed God in some way. God's will for our lives is to live in peace. Anyone who lives together but endures continuous hurt, anger and is convinced that all of these negative emotions are their spouse's fault, are just as divorced as the couple that hires an attorney and calls it quits. A covenant marriage is one that demonstrates the ability to love unconditionally and freely. For this reason, Jesus said, "What therefore *God* has joined together, let no man put asunder" (Mark 10:9; Matt. 19:6).

The challenge of applying the word to our lives is searching the scriptures for ourselves.

Motivational Scriptures:

But be sure to fear the Lord and serve him faithfully with all your heart; consider what great things he has done for you.
(I Sam. 12:2)

"Remember O Lord, how I have walked before you faithfully and with wholeheartedly devotion and have done what is good in your eyes..."
(2 Kings 20:3)

But the fruit of the spirit is love, joy, peace, patience, kindness, goodness, faithfulness, gentleness and self-control.
(Gal. 5:22-23)

Dear Abby

Abigail Van Buren is a noted newspaper columnist that has been around for more years than many of us, perhaps even our mothers and surely some of our grandmothers can recall. You can find her responding via her weekly advice column to countless correspondences from people of all ages, genders and cultural backgrounds. The letters she receives are extremely diverse and I am convinced that it takes years of wisdom and experience to respond in the insightful way that she does. Perhaps with age comes wisdom. With that statement you will find no argument from me. However, I think it is also equally important to note that experience is also an awesome teacher.

I do not know Abigail Van Buren personally; therefore, I do not know her life's experiences though I have read her column "Dear Abby" on numerous occasions (for entertainment purposes only, of course). I have found most of her advice quite levelheaded, for what it's worth. At least that is what her column reveals, though I do not view her as a prophetess, royal priestess or possessing divine authority from on high by any means. Furthermore, I do not exactly know what qualifies Abigail Van Buren to administer the advice she gives. Perhaps Abigail Van Buren's life experiences have given her such authority to emanate such assumed wisdom. Perhaps to do so is Abigail Van Buren's gift and she is merely operating in it. God Bless her and her giftedness if this is the case.

Yet, there is another Abigail I would like to introduce to some and present to others, Abigail, the wife of Nabal. A Hebrew woman. A godly woman. A woman described by Bible scholars as possessing influence, beauty and wisdom. A woman whose name means, " my father rejoiced", while her husband's name means "fool". Yet she intervened on her husband Nabal's behalf in humble submission to God (1Samuel 25:2-42). I'm sure if we were able to sit and write this Abigail a letter or two or have the good fortune of having her respond to our most intimate inquiries, Abigail's insight and wisdom would be more than any modern day newspaper columnist, TV psychic, or soothsayer could ever impart.

Woman of God, imagine being disappointed by your spouse because he has made a bad decision. Perhaps he has spent the remaining balance in the checking account, forgot to tell you, and now you have to beat the check you wrote on your joint account to the bank. Perhaps he has caused a riff between you and your family. He made a promise he did not keep and has left you to face the person whom he has disappointed. He spoke out of turn and offended your parents. He gambled away the mortgage payment the day before it was due. He misunderstood your commitment to serving God and your church. In turn he has belligerently confronted your Pastor and other members of the congregation, causing you major embarrassment. He has had a run in with the law and now you have found yourself pleading with the judge or magistrate on his behalf.

I know your first inclination may be to think, Gee-Wiz! A God fearing man would not put himself or his family in such a predicament! Well, I heard someone say that a Saint is just a sinner who fell down. Even those persons whom we hold in high esteem are vulnerable to making reckless misjudgments at sometime in their lives. Look at some of our world leaders in the very recent past. If presidents, civil rights activists preachers and pastors can fall, so can our mates, some are our mates and so can we. Just like the Hebrew woman Abigail, our place is to be the helpmates God has called us to be, standing in the gap, ready, willing and able to do what God has told wives to do. No matter what the costs. For as long as God commands it.

What advice can we glean from this woman Abigail? First of all, as we seek wise counsel from our ally, we must first do the femininely inspired obvious thing. Examine this sister's character:

- ❖ *<u>Abigail possessed sound character that was made evident by the way she ministered to her marriage in the midst of conflict.</u>*
  Abigail's reputation for being a good wife obviously preceded her. Nabal's servants knew that his wife would know what to do in the midst of his irrational behavior.

- ❖ *<u>Abigail was respected and trusted by her husband's servants.</u>*

  The servants came to her, which reveals the deep trust and confidence they had in her. Once Abigail heard of her husband's idiocy, she acts immediately, yet with wisdom. Who do you know whose first reaction to learning of their husband's bad judgments would be to immediately fly off the handle only to make matters worse? I would imagine this was not the first time Abigail found herself having to save face as a result of Nabal's foolish decisions. However, it was the way she carried herself in the past that let Nabal's men know that she would represent her husband well in the face of an incensed David.

- ❖ *<u>Abigail was very bold in the midst of an intimidating situation.</u>*

  My sister, do you not know sometimes you will just have to square your back, wipe your weeping eyes and go boldly before the adversary in Jesus' name? (Prov. 28:1). Abigail has proven herself to be a woman of integrity and practical experience. I'm sure she would counsel any woman who has found herself faced with the challenges of sticking it out to just do what God has asked and given you strength to do. The problem is we are so busy trying to work everything out ourselves, God cannot show up and show out for Himself. He has your back! He can do what you cannot do! You just do what you can. He will do the rest! Though her husband behaved foolishly, she did not wallow in self-pity, she did what she knew to do regardless of her circumstances. I'm convinced Abigail, the Hebrew woman would advise us that our advancement in life will depend on our character. What was it that caused Nabal to react the way he did? Was it that his pride got the best of him? Was it after hearing Abigail's account of her meeting with David he realized what a dangerous position he had placed those who were so close to him in? His heart couldn't take it.

If we diligently research the 25th chapter of I Samuel, we will see with our mind's eye that God has a way of removing foolishness out of our lives and replacing it with greatness. In Abigail's situation, it was David, a fearless leader who later became a King after God's own heart. In your situation, it could very well be your own husband. God did say, "Therefore if any man be in Christ, he is a new creature: old things are past away; behold, all things are become new." (II Cor. 5:17) If your mate is in Christ, he can become new. He can become your King! If he is not in Christ (saved), pray that he will be opened to receiving Jesus Christ as his Lord and Savior right now.

Women are elevated to new levels in Christ because of their character in the midst of their husband's follies. The Holy Spirit will clue you in on how long to endure if you find yourself about to throw in the towel. Keep in mind; you alone will never be able to change your husband. Only God can do that. What you can do is keep him lifted before the Lord. This may require fasting as well as prayer. Make a positive change to the way you will react to what your husband does. This can be accomplished with the Lord's guidance and Holy intervention. (Matt. 6:33, Prov. 3:5-6)

Do you recall Effie Barry the ex-wife of the former Mayor of Washington, D.C., Marion Barry? Jacqueline

Jackson, the dedicated wife of Civil Rights Activist, the Reverend Jesse Jackson, and even former First Lady and current New York State Senator, Hillary Rodham-Clinton, the wife of our nation's 42nd President, William Jefferson "Bill" Clinton? There are countless other women who stood with dignity beside their husbands in the face of public scorn and ridicule I am sure.   These women maintained God-like character in spite of the fact that modern day society, the media and perhaps even their own peers would have them perform otherwise for the entire world to see. Like any other person who has given these women any thought, these women had their weak moments behind closed doors without a doubt. Nonetheless, they stood publicly with integrity and grace. What's more, God, yes God has elevated them to higher heights. Now is the time to take on the posture of boldness in your marriage. You must live with an attitude laced with the kind of virtuosity that will make your heavenly father rejoice- An Abigail spirit!

A Humble Wife's Prayer

Father, in the name of Jesus, I present myself before You in total obedience and humble submission. I pray for Your forgiveness for not always being obedient to Your word. I invite You into my life and most importantly every crack and crevice of my circumstances. Lord, help me to be the woman of God You have made me. Help me to totally surrender to You and to be still and know that You are God.

I know I cannot change my spouse, however, I do know through prayer and with your help, the both of us can become new creatures. A right spirit can be renewed within us if we would just humble our selves before You. I can possess an Abigail spirit and my husband can become my King!

Lord, I believe You are able to deposit within me a desire for positive self-change and the wisdom to let Your will be done in my husband's life.

I know You and only You Lord are the one who can cure the "dis-eases" we are experiencing in our marriage. Keep my thoughts from picking away at the scabs that are covering the sore emotional areas in our marriage and apply your healing balm to make us well.

I trust and believe in Your power to grant my every request in Your time, in Your loving and merciful way.

Thank You in advance as I patiently wait upon Your response.

In Jesus' Name,
Amen!

Find The Meaning In Ministering To Your Spouse

The following exercises are designed to help you and your spouse inventory your individual and joint strengths-as well as evaluate your needs and the needs around you-as a first step in the process of finding the meaning in your marriage.

1. What emotional, intellectual, social, or spiritual needs do you see in your spouse?

2. Are there any ways you could minister to your spouse by meeting those needs? If so, how?

Needs	How Can I Minister?

3) What strengths and weaknesses do you each bring to your marriage? In what ways do these strengths and weaknesses interact so that you complement each other?

I'm Strong	I'm Weak

Spouse Strong	Spouse Weak

Ways We Complement Each Other:

4) What goals can each of you accomplish-either individually or together-because of your marriage that you couldn't accomplish alone? What opportunities can you respond to?

Goals	Opportunities

5) What needs can you meet- or what problems can you overcome-by being together? (Eccl. 4:9)

Needs/Problems   **How To Overcome Them**

6) What ministry do you and your spouse have to your children? What hopes, dreams, and goals do you have for your children that you can work on in your marriage?

Emotional   **Intellectual**

Social   **Spiritual**

7) What strengths and weaknesses do you and your spouse bring to your marriage that affect your ministry to your children?

I'm Strong   **I'm Weak**

Spouse Is Strong   **Spouse Is Weak**

8) What opportunities, problems, or threats related to your children can you and your spouse respond to together? How?

Problems/Opportunities/ Threats   **How To Respond**

9) What needs exist in your church, your community, and the larger world, which you are able to do something about and want to do something about? List needs that you can better address because you are married or that you can address in partnership with your spouse.

Needs   **How to Address Them**

10) What strengths and weaknesses do you and your spouse bring to your marriage that are relevant to your ministry to the church and to the larger world?

I'm Strong   **I'm Weak**

Spouse Is Strong   **Spouse Is Weak**

11) Write a mission statement for your marriage, keeping in mind the various chapters you have read in this book.

Journaling

Begin to keep a journal to document how you see God working in your life to bring you to holiness and wholeness. How is God calling you to minister to your spouse? Be specific about how you see God working.

❖ Richard Matteson. Janis Long Harris, What If I Married the Wrong Person (Minneapolis, Minnesota: Bethany House Publishers, 1996) 246-249

Another Tenth Commandment

I believe Bishop Vashti Murphy McKenzie; the first female Bishop elected in the African Methodist Episcopal Church put it best in her book, *Not Without a Struggle. Leadership Development for African American Women in Ministry.* In her book she lists what associate women ministers and pastors in the Methodist and Baptist traditions describe as the Ten Womanist Commandments for clergywomen. The tenth of these commandments read as follows:

10. <u>THOU SHALL NOT TAKE THYSELF TOO SERIOUSLY</u>

"Though shall have a sense of humor," said one suburban pastor. "Thou shall frequently do a self-examination," said another.

Nothing lasts forever. The seasons do change. New ones will rush in with their own set of distinctions and characteristics. Learn to laugh a little to yourself and with others. Play a little to balance your workload.

Walk, jump, run, swim, and eat and sleep right. Stop to smell the roses and to take hot bubble baths.

Maintenance is just as important as the mission. If a car is not properly maintained-with oil changes, tune-ups, gas in the tank, and air in the tires-it will not go far and run well.

If all of that is too hard to grasp when you are trying to balance responsibilities to God, husband, children, school, job, denominational officials, and significant others, just remember these four words of Rev. Cecelia Williams Bryant: "Relax, Retreat, Reflect, and Renew." [3]

While you meditate on the chapters you have read in this book, the scriptures you have discovered and revisited, the prayers you have prayed as you learn to do as God has asked, you may feel a bit overwhelmed and feel the need for just a little more time to take all of this in. Perhaps you are not married clergy or feel divinely called to pastoral ministry. On the other hand, you just may feel a bit more energized and ready to tackle the day, full steam ahead! Whatever the present state of mind or condition we find ourselves in, we can all stand to take ourselves a little less seriously.

Yes, marriage is serious business and is not to be entered in to unadvisedly or to be taken lightly. At times it may seem that God has put married women in such an unfair position. There is so much work to do. However, there is no need to completely stress yourself out doing it. Once you learn to forgive and discontinue to nurture past hurts and offenses, the load will lessen. After all, we serve a merciful God who forgives each one of us, whether we deserve it or not. That is how God honors the covenant He has made with us.

Know this for yourselves- with God all things are possible for the Mrs. who ministers to her marriage.

Be encouraged! Be Blessed!

Appendix

The following are several scenarios that seem to be most common as couples have shared issues that challenge their marriages. Read each one carefully. If you find that any of these scenarios apply to you and your marriage, I pray you will search the scriptures suggested by the author and seek God's instruction to promote healing for your situation.

1) My mate is not the same person I thought I married___ years ago. He/She no longer seems to meet my expectations.
Lam. 3:22, John 13:35, Rom. 8:38-39

2) My mate often says, "I will do this for you, if you will do that for me."
I Corin. 7:3-4, Eph. 2:19, Gal. 3:26-29, Prov. 2:17, Malachi 2:14

3) My mate and I never seem to see things eye to eye.
Amos 3:3, Eccl. 4:8,9

4) It seems as though I possess more spiritual maturity than my spouse.
Ps. 139:13-14, I Cor. 12:4-5, Gen. 2:20-23

5) Our in-laws, friends and acquaintances seem to have more influence in our household than what's necessary.
Gen. 2:24, Mark 3:31-35, Eph. 4:2

6) My husband/wife seems to think that I should do whatever he/she says.
   Phil. 2:1-4, Eph. 5:21-33, Prov. 18:2

7) I wish my mate were more encouraging and disagreed with me less often.
   I Cor. 13:4, Prov. 18:13, 21, I Peter 3:4

Has your outlook on your relationship changed as a result of these scriptures? __Yes ___No. If yes, how? If no, prayerfully read Romans 12:2 until the scriptures become comprehensible to you.

*How Much Responsibility Are **You** Willing to Take For the Enrichment of Your Marriage?*

This book has not been written with the intent to replace professional counseling. Though it is the author's belief that God is the ultimate healer of relationship matters. God has given us the gift of trained, qualified professionals to assist us while we yet remain here on earth.

- ❖ **National Domestic Violence Hotline: 1-800-799-SAFE (7233)**
  The National Domestic Violence Hotline is staffed twenty-four hours a day by trained counselors who can provide crisis assistance and information about local shelters, legal support, health care centers and clinics and additional counseling in your area.

- ❖ The U.S. Department of Health and Human Services (HHS) Substance Abuse and Mental Health Services Administration (SAMHSA) National Drug and Treatment Referral Routing Service provides a toll-free telephone number for alcohol and drug information/treatment referral assistance. They can be reach by calling: 1-800-662-HELP.

- ❖ For a referral to a psychologist in your area, consult your local clergy or call: 1-800-964-2000. The operator will need your zip code to locate and connect you with the referral system in your area.

- ❖ Your employer also may offer an Employee Assistance Program (EAP) through your healthcare insurance provider. Check with the Human Resource Benefit Manager at your place of employment.

Notes

1 Stormie Omartian, The Power of A Praying Husband (Eugene, Oregon: Harvest House Publishers, 2001) 164

2 Jerry B. Jenkins, Loving Your Marriage Enough To Protect It (Chicago, IL: Moody Press, 1993) 61

3 Vashti M. McKenzie, Not Without A Struggle. Leadership Development for African American Women in Ministry (Cleveland, Ohio: Pilgrim Press, 1996) 115

4 Dr. Richard Matteson and Janis Long Harris, What If I Married the Wrong Person? (Minneapolis, Minnesota: Bethany House Publishers, 1996) 246-249

ABOUT THE AUTHOR

Minister Zenola Diggs is a native of Flint, Michigan. She and her husband, Minister Rodney K. Diggs of nine years have lived in Nashville, Tennessee since 1997 and are Associate Ministers overseeing the Marriage Enrichment Ministry at one of the fastest growing churches in the state of Tennessee, the Mt. Zion Baptist Church with a membership of over 7,000 members. She became a Licensed Minister of the Gospel in 1999 under the covering of Mt. Zion's Senior Pastor, Bishop Joseph W. Walker III, D.Min. Minister Diggs has been recognized to obtain ordained eldership. Minister Diggs has several years of Christian Education experience in the United Methodist Church as a certified Lay Speaker and within the Full Gospel Baptist Church. She has served in the music and Christian education ministries as well as and conducting various workshops, seminars and annual Marriage

Enrichment Conferences alongside her husband.

Minister Zenola Diggs holds a Bachelors Degree in Marketing Management and Communication from the University of Michigan. She has completed Graduate studies in Marriage and Family Therapy at Trevecca Nazarene University in Nashville. She is also a member of the American Association of Christian Counslors. Minister Diggs is currently pursuing joint Masters and Doctorate degrees in Christian Counseling from Andersonville Baptist Seminary in Camilla, Georgia and is the co-founder of One Flesh Ministries, Inc. She has also appeared on Nashville's Christian television show Bridges on WHTN-TV 39 and the Trinity Broadcast Network (TBN).

You may contact Minister Zenola Diggs at email address: mindiggs@yahoo.com or LightHouse Press, P.O. Box 281375, Nashville, Tennessee 37228